Executive Summary

Title: Moral Fitness: Ethical Education for Marines

Author: Major Michael T. Hlad, United States Marine Corps

Thesis: Through integrated leadership and ethics education in the leadership continuum, the Marine Corps can create a resilient and ethical force better prepared for the moral dilemmas of combat operations, military service, and life after the military.

Discussion: The Marine Corps has ethical foundations embedded in its training and history. Exploring the Marine Corps values and how they form our ethical foundation, we can see how important it is for the Marine Corps to have an ethical force. The importance of ethics in the Marine Corps is published in its doctrine, but the institutional approach to ethics fails to integrate ethics education across the Marine Corps. What we teach for ethics, how we teach it and where it is taught has a direct impact on the actions of our leaders and Marines. The Marine Corps needs to make key changes to create an effective ethical force: Develop an ethical vision for the Marine Corps, focused ethical education, and moral fitness.

Conclusion: Embracing this dedication to a new moral fitness prepares our Marines for the toughest situations and teaches them how to deal with the ethical dilemmas we know they will face in combat. This is done by educating them in the formal schools, re-enforcing these teachings in training, and making those teachings a habit in our day-to-day responsibilities. This refocusing and strategic educational guidance is critical to the future of the Marine Corps. Educating our Marines on ethical and moral teachings will serve the Marine Corps for decades to come.

DISCLAIMER

THE OPINIONS AND CONCLUSIONS EXPRESSED HEREIN ARE THOSE OF THE INDIVIDUAL STUDENT AUTHOR AND DO NOT NECESSARILY REPRESENT THE VIEWS OF EITHER THE MARINE CORPS COMMAND AND STAFF COLLEGE OR ANY OTHER GOVERNMENTAL AGENCY. REFERENCES TO THIS STUDY SHOULD INCLUDE THE FOREGOING STATEMENT.

QUOTATION FROM, ABSTRACTION FROM, OR REPRODUCTION OF ALL OR ANY PART OF THIS DOCUMENT IS PERMITTED PROVIDED PROPER ACKNOWLEDGEMENT IS MADE.

Illustrations

Page

Figure 1. Kohlberg's scale of moral development...11

Figure 2. Marine Corps: Leadership Development Continua...13

Figure 3. Proposed ethical development model...13

Table of Contents

Page

Title page i

Executive summary ii

Disclaimer iii

Illustrations iv

Table of Contents v

Preface vi

Introduction/Background 1

Section 1: Ethics and the Marine Corps 5

Section 2: Marine Corps core values 6

Section 3: Education 8

Section 4: Training 15

Section 5: What needs to change 18

Conclusion 20

Citations and endnotes 22

Bibliography 23

Preface

One of the first things a new Marine learns is that they rarely do anything alone — it is most often a team effort. Fortunately for me, outstanding individuals have helped me complete this journey in exploring the Marine Corps and ethical education.

First, my wonderful wife, who manages to balance all of the sacrifices required of a military spouse as well as have her own successful career. Thank you for listening, critiquing, and helping me on this journey. I could not have a better partner. You understand the Marine Corps and me, and I appreciate your continued and unwavering support and love.

To the leadership and ethics team at the Naval Academy: You inspired me to focus on my own ethical education as well as the Marine Corps'. CAPT James Campbell, Col. Art Athens, and LtCol Joseph Thomas, your teachings have inspired thousands of midshipmen and officers in the Navy and Marine Corps. I consider myself extremely fortunate to have been educated by such great officers and teachers. CAPT Campbell challenged us daily in our Moral Obligations class, which was inspired by the great Admiral Jim Stockdale. Those lessons are what fueled my passion for ethics and looking at how we could do better in the Marine Corps. Thank you, gentlemen, for continuing to instill the important lessons of ethics and life in our future leaders.

To my Command and Staff mentors, Dr. Rebecca Johnson, Dr. Richard Dinardo, and Cdr Russell Evans: Thank you for your continued effort to improve the Marine Corps through the education of its officers. You have challenged my thought process and enhanced my view of the Marine Corps, as well as the future of warfare. Dr. Johnson, thank you for your passion for ethics and for challenging me through this research process. I could not have completed this without your continuous feedback and hard work.

*Sound morals and ethical behavior cannot be established or created in a day...
a semester... or a year. They must be institutionalized within our character over
time... they must become a way of life. They go beyond our individual services
and beyond our ranks or positions, they cut to the heart and to the soul of who
we are and what we are and what we must be...men and women of character.
They arm us for the challenges to come and they impart to us a sense of wholeness.
They unite us in the calling we now know as the profession of arms.*

-General Charles C. Krulak, Keynote Address, Joint Service Conference on Ethics, 2000 [1]

Introduction:

The United States has been involved in combat operations for the past decade. Some of

the darkest moments in those conflicts have come from the ethical failings of some of our service

members. The Marine Corps prides itself on maintaining high ethical standards; however, we are

not immune to these failings — as seen by the body desecration video and SS flag photos in

Afghanistan. These failings have occurred during times of high operational tempo and have

caused Marine Corps leadership, the public, and civilian leaders to question our ethical

foundations and training. What can the Marine Corps do to create Marines who are ethical when

it matters the most? Through integrated leadership and ethics education in the leadership

continuum, the Marine Corps can create a resilient and ethical force better prepared for the moral

dilemmas of combat operations, military service, and life after the military.

This paper will focus on three areas: what the Marine Corps currently conducts for moral

development, the formal ways the Marine Corps looks to educate and train an ethical force, and

suggestions for modifying current professional military education and training with the relevant

ethical education to further enhance the Marine Corps.

1

Background:

As America and the military begin to transition from a decade of war, it is vital that the Marine Corps continue to develop leaders prepared for the moral and ethical challenges of military service. Recent incidents have forced this issue to a national discussion and are changing the perceptions of the modern military force. From Iraq to Afghanistan, unethical decisions can have strategic ramifications, causing our political leaders and military commanders to react and to events, instead of focusing on the campaign or war.

In 2012, the Marine Corps faced two incidents that struck at the moral fiber of what it means to be a Marine. The Commandant of the Marine Corps, Gen. Jim Amos, responded to these incidents, Marines urinating on Taliban bodies and Marine snipers posing in front of an "SS" flag, with a month-long ethical stand down across the Marine Corps, including its general officers. The Commandant acknowledged, "We have a problem here," and published a white letter in March 2012, titled "Leadership and Conduct." It called for a new emphasis on accountability and discipline within the Marine Corps at all levels. In a *Marine Corps Times* article, Gen. Amos said, "We are allowing our standards to erode; recent missteps indicate there is complacency by some in the enforcement of our own high standards. The high regard of our fellow citizens and our own self-image are at stake."[2] The Commandant is correct that the Marine Corps must continue to have the trust and confidence of the American people.

The military continues to be one of the most trusted institutions in American society, according to recent studies; however, recent events have caused the leadership to evaluate the training provided to the force.[3] The Marine Corps must continue to strive to provide the nation with warriors who can meet the demands of combat environments without sacrificing their ethical foundations. Leon Panetta, former Secretary of Defense, addressed this issue to the senior military leadership in a letter on March 2, 2012.[4] He stated, "Ethical culture must remain a priority in the days ahead; as it is essential to sustaining the trust America places in her Armed Forces. This trust is foundational to the Department's ability to protect our Nation."[5]

As Marines continue to be engaged in combat operations around the globe, the life and death dilemmas they face are similar to those that previous generations faced. The Mental Health Advisory Team IV (MHAT) published a report on November 17, 2006, on information gathered through the Office of the Surgeon General to assess the mental health and well-being of soldiers and Marines. The report had some troubling statistics, particularly for the Marine Corps. It found that a third of Marines (31%) stated that they did not know how to respond when facing ethical dilemmas in combat in Iraq.[6] Despite stating that they had received ethical training, they still felt they were unprepared for the situations they would face in combat. The report showed a direct correlation between combat experiences and unethical behavior. The MHAT recommended that military leaders increase battlefield ethics training in preparation for the complex environment the Marines and soldiers are facing.

If there is an instruction manual for the Marine Corps, it is Victor Krulak's book, *First to Fight*, which is required reading for all Marines. It lays out the history, legacy, and traditions of Marines established through the examples of Marines in World War II, Korea, and Vietnam. This book provides modem Marines examples of ethical decisions made in combat. Today, Marines must use these examples and help mold a modern effective force with a sound ethical foundation. The Marine Corps has no single document or doctrine that resembles an overarching ethical roadmap, and it is up to the educational institutions to determine their ethics curriculum and focus. We are lacking an ethical developmental model that helps Marines focus on what to teach, which theories to focus on, and the appropriate level of development to help to facilitate education for an ethical force.

There is a debate on whether an effective ethical military force is possible. Some would argue that military effectiveness and ethics will ultimately conflict. Martin Cook, for example, looked at disciplinary records at the United States Air Force Academy and the habits developed through rewards and punishments. The process, which is common for the military academies, intended to train cadets to develop the right habits that are justified functionally, yet they are given lectures with the intention of improving their moral aspirations.[7] While this warrants more debate, a purely functional approach is not consistent with the higher aims of military service. Marines are morally responsible professionals serving an important moral good, and the Marine Corps must be committed to educating Marines to the ethical ends they should aspire to attain. Given the current operational picture, the Marine Corps must adopt an aspirational approach, which means significant changes in training and education are needed to maintain high ethical standards. Focusing on ethical education will demonstrate a sincere commitment from the Marine Corps to create a force that acknowledges and understands the ethical constraints of military force.[8]

Focusing on theories of moral character and ethical education, the Marine Corps can aim to develop Marines who are effective and prepared to make the right and just decisions. The goal should be to develop individual Marines and treat them as their own moral agents who are responsible for their rational decisions, moral reflection, and moral change. A functional approach teaches the ethical lessons but ignores the ramifications on the individual Marine, who has to live with his actions on the battlefield. This does not represent the Marine Corps' intent or commitment to the individual Marine. A more aspirational approach, an approach that focuses on ethical foundations, leads to internal decision-making versus external influences. This will maintain the Marine Corps' public image as an honorable profession while demonstrating a sincere commitment to the ethical decision-making and development of the individual Marine.[9]

Section1: Ethics and the Marine Corps

The Marine Corps does not have one document that defines "ethics" directly; however, ethical decision making is intertwined with our history, doctrine, and training. The real foundation of the Marin Corps ethos is the core values of honor, courage, and commitment. This "ethos" is described in foundational documents like Marine Corps Doctrinal Publication (MCDP) 1, *First to Fight* and the *Small Wars Manual.* Through these foundational documents, the Marine Corps "ethos" is described and heritage demonstrates this "ethos" in action.

Ethics means many things to many people, and when incorporating ethics into a military setting, it becomes increasingly complex due to the nature and challenges of war. Ethics is the study of philosophy that addresses questions about morality.[10] Often, ethics is known as moral philosophy and deals with concepts of good and bad, right and wrong, and good and evil. The word "ethics" derives from the Greek term "ethos," better translated as "character," where "morality" comes from the Latin term "mos," which refers to character habits and is essentially the same concept. Although there are intellectual disagreements on the differences of the meanings, this paper will use ethics. Deciding on the right thing is not always easy, and ethics often involves choosing the hard right rather than the easier wrong, or sometimes choosing between two hard rights. A moral dilemma is when two or more deeply held values clash. This is common in Marine combat scenarios, where Marines may have to choose between the safety of their fellow Marines, the integrity of a mission, and ensuring innocent lives are not lost. The MHAT survey gives us the troubling reality that a third of our Marines did not know how to respond to certain moral situations. Solving these tough dilemmas requires a sound foundation in understanding ethical principles and the impacts of the chosen solutions.[11]

The Marine Corps looks to solve moral dilemmas by instilling ethics through the key virtues of honor, courage, and commitment early in a Marine's career. This ethos is enforced during the indoctrination process, when Marines are taught that they have to do the right thing even during the toughest situations. They can not torture prisoners, attack innocent civilians, and they must re-enforce the key values and uphold the honor and traditions of the Marine Corps.

Section 2: Marine Corps core values

> *This high name of distinction and soldierly repute, we who are Marines today have received from those who preceded us in the Corps. With it, we also received from them the eternal spirit which has animated our Corps from generation to generation and has been the distinguishing mark of the Marines in every age.*
> *Major General John A. Lejeune, 10 November 1921[12]*

To further evaluate these core Marine Corps values, we must look at where they derive from and what they mean. How are honor, courage, and commitment codified into the Marine Corps structure? What is the Marine Corps' goal in these service values? This section explores these core values and how they apply to the ethical foundation of the Marine Corps, including how they are expressed individually and at the unit level, and why this is important to the culture of the Marine Corps.

Marines are indoctrinated into the culture of the Marine Corps at a recruit depot or at Officer Candidates School. This indoctrination is not only the training on how to effectively be a Marine, physical fitness, combat tatics, and weapon proficiency, but also what it means to be a Marine: the ethos of the Marine Corps. One of the first classes for these new Marines is the core values of the institution: honor, courage, and commitment. These lessons instill a sense of responsibility in new Marines from day one, and underscore the importance of these values.

These values are codified in Marine Corps order 1500.56, published in 1996, which outlines the Marine Corps values and their implementation throughout the Marine Corps. To further state this point, Gen. Charles Krulak, then the Commandant of the Marine Corps, said, "There is no room in the Marine Corps for situational ethics or situational morality."[13] Each Marine is expected to be a man or women of character, grounded in the Marine Corps' core values.

The Marine Corps focuses on the character traits associated with each value. The definitions of these core values are important, as they represent the Corps' ethical foundation:

Honor. Marines set the standard for conduct for our society both at home and abroad and they do this by demonstrating four elements of honor as described by the Marine Corps values guide. One, by demonstrating integrity by doing what is right, legal, and ethical. For being accountable for one's actions, understanding that one Marine's actions can save the day in a situation and makes the Marine Corps team stronger. Marines do not lie, cheat, or steal and honesty is a standard among all Marines. Finally, that through the respect of past traditions, and respect for those that have gone before them, Marines are to embody integrity and ethical behavior every day. [14]

Courage. The "moral, mental, and physical strength to resist opposition, face danger, and endure hardship..."[15] This concept of courage is demonstrated by the following characteristics that are taught to Marines. Self-discipline, which Marines are accountable for their actions and hold others accountable for their actions as well. A Marine is dedicated to maintaining the moral and mental health and to exercise the pursuit of knowledge. Having the steadfast loyalty through service to the Corps, one's command, one's fellow Marines, self, and family. Valor through one's determination to confront the dangers of battle and service and every Marine is committed to excellence and knowledge in all of their actions.

Commitment. The ability for Marines to promise that they will accomplish the mission through worthy means by demonstrating actions in support of this goal through these characteristics. Setting a high standard of excellence through competency and teamwork. Through teamwork, individual Marines work to support the larger mission, while always taking care of each other. Marines are selfless, they are committed to taking care of others, subordinates, peers, and individual welfare is second to the importance of the country and the Marine Corps. Marine's are custodians for the nation's future, the people, and to defend the nation and ideals of honorable citizens, no matter the race, religion, political stance, gender or the individual Marine. Finally, that a Marine understands of the ideals of the constitution and the rights and duties in one's oath of service, that the ideals in embodied in this document gives the individual Marine a source of strength that they can draw upon during times of battle and hardship.[16]

These elements of honor, courage, and commitment embody the character and ethos that the Marine Corps wants in its Marines. It is so important that at one time Marines were ordered to carry "Honor, Courage, Commitment" cards so that they would remember what it means to be a Marine. This character drives a Marine's decision-making process in particular situations, as described in Marine Corps Order 1500.56 and the Marine Corps values program.[17]

The Marine Corps' values of honor, courage, and commitment are important to the indoctrination, identity, and character of the Marine Corps and the individual Marine. However, core values training is not enough. These values, as they have been expressed and defined, must become a habit for the individual Marine, so he or she makes the right decisions for the right reasons. As Aristotle noted, one cannot develop virtue by accident — one must acquire these traits by habit.

Section 3: Education

Core values are important and set an important foundation, but they do little by themselves to provide Marines with the framework for making these tough decisions. Think of the MHAT survey that showed Marines were unclear on what to do when their values were challenged. The core values are an important starting block of an ethical framework that is integrated into our military education curriculum. However, the Marine Corps is failing to fully integrate and educate Marines on ethics in the classroom and missing a great opportunity to enhance and prepare Marines outside of the classroom.

The Marine Corps has placed renewed emphasis on professional military education, specifically for the officer corps, at the flagship for Marine Corps education, Marine Corps University in Quantico, Virginia. Specifically, The Basic School (TBS), Expeditionary Warfare School (EWS), Command and Staff college (CSC), the School of Advanced Warfighting (SAW) and the Marine Corps War College (MCWAR), where the Marine Corps trains Lieutenants (TBS), Captains (EWS), Majors (CSC & SAW) and Lieutenant Colonels (MCWAR). These schools have recently conducted a curriculum review and are incorporating more ethical education; however, they lack the horizontal integration and coordination for a cohesive ethical continuum.

Each of these schools dedicates a "package," or lessons, on ethics. Each school focuses on preparing for command, developing subordinates at different levels, ethics and law of war, and the human element of combat. The goal of the specific lessons is to build on the students' foundation of character based on leadership while preparing them for the challenges of future assignments across the spectrum of conflict.[18]

While these schools may vary in approach and focus, their application of ethics is varied, and there is no clear ethical development plan applied to all Marines across the many formal schools. Such a plan must also include the Staff Non Commissioned Officer (SNCO) Academy, the Non Commissioned Officer (NCO) courses, senior level schools like the War College and General officers, to facilitate all Marines, at every rank.

The SNCOs and junior officers will have the largest impact on the formation of junior enlisted Marines. Clinton Culp, in his chapter in *Aspects of Leadership*, examines current pedagogical methods in the military. He points out that the Lieutenants, Captains, and Staff Non Commissioned Officers are in the ideal positions to conduct character education in the operational forces, if they are equipped with the proper tools; however, he points out that character education does not equal training, and a more deliberate effort to equip these service members with an ethical foundation. Only then can they make the important links to ethics when making decisions, of one's conduct and the core values of the organization.[19]

In addition to focusing on ethical education, Mr. Culp states that military members must take into account the moral sophistication of the individual. For example, two 18-year-old enlisted Marines could be at two different levels of reasoning, just like two Captains or seasoned veterans. He asserts that the older one is, the more life experience one has, and the more education, critical thinking and reasoning skills one has, the more sophisticated that person's moral reasoning will be.[20] Currently, a Marine may only have an opportunity to attend a formal school every three to four years if he is selected and the Marine Corps does not require all Marines to attend these schools. Not only do we fail to educate some of our Marines on these important principals, it is not re-enforced in the fleet Marine force.

The standard for moral development has been Lawrence Kohlberg's theory, which is an adaptation conceived from the Swiss psychologist Jean Piaget. Kohlberg's theory on moral reasoning, the basis of ethical behavior, has six identifiable developmental stages. Each of the developmental stages builds upon the other, with each stage more adequate at responding to moral dilemmas than its predecessor. Depicted in the following image is the model for Kohlberg's moral development theory:

Photo Removed Due to Copyright Restrictions

Kohlberg grouped his stages of moral development into three levels: the pre-conventional, the conventional level, and the post conventional. According to Kohlberg, most adults stop developing in the conventional level. This puts the challenge on the Marine Corps to develop junior Marines to think in terms of at least level 2, Stage 4 (Societal Expectations and doing one's duty). It is also important to note a study conducted by LtCol Kenneth Williams on moral reasoning and development. LtCol Williams found that during a nine-week entry-level training program, moral reasoning is not affected by the education process and in some cases decreases.[21] If the Marine Corps believes boot camp alone will instill the values and ethics it wants displayed in combat, scientific studies have shown otherwise. We must integrate ethical education for our junior Marines, as they are the ones who are on the front lines and faced with the toughest life-or-death decisions. This would point to more training for enlisted Marines following boot camp, both formal and informal.

The key is to understand the various stages in Kohlberg's moral development and to identify what levels we want to focus on and study how we can best educate them. Few individuals attain the levels of Stage 5 or 6 in Kohlberg's moral motivation, but understanding the levels and schemas of moral reasoning allows the educator and the Marine Corps to ask the appropriate "why" question in the classroom and establish an appropriate curriculum for a course.[22]

The goal would be to teach these Marines to exercise moral reasoning and make ethical decisions not in terms of their common peer groups, but in terms of the Marine Corps' societal expectations. [23] Understanding the mindset of the 18- to 24-year-old enlistee and the pressures they have on loyalty to their peer group versus the obligation to the institution is an important dynamic to discuss and explore. This level of ethical thinking would serve the Marine Corps and the individual Marine, as they would have a sound understanding of right and wrong as well as an understanding of the consequences of failing to do the right thing in the context of the Marine Corps and society. This early foundation, continually re-enforced through follow-on education, will serve the Marines when they are in combat and being truly tested.

These phases of moral development can be applied to our current leadership continua as established by the Lejeune Leadership Institute pictured below. As you will see there is no clear line dedicated to ethics. We must modify this model to account for the ethical development of the Marine Corps.

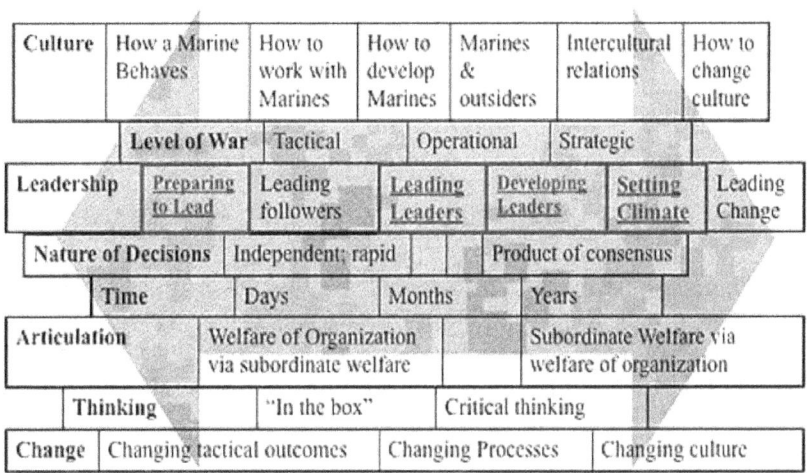

Culture	How a Marine Behaves	How to work with Marines	How to develop Marines	Marines & outsiders	Intercultural relations	How to change culture

Level of War	Tactical		Operational	Strategic

Leadership	Preparing to Lead	Leading followers	Leading Leaders	Developing Leaders	Setting Climate	Leading Change

Nature of Decisions	Independent; rapid		Product of consensus

Time	Days	Months	Years

Articulation	Welfare of Organization via subordinate welfare		Subordinate Welfare via welfare of organization

Thinking	"In the box"	Critical thinking

Change	Changing tactical outcomes	Changing Processes	Changing culture

Utilizing Kohlberg's model, previous research, and the ethics model by LtCol Patterson and Phipps, this proposed model can be incorporated into the leadership continuum or as its own continua to be built upon.

This model incorporates Kohlberg's stages and pairs them with the formal Marine Corps schools.

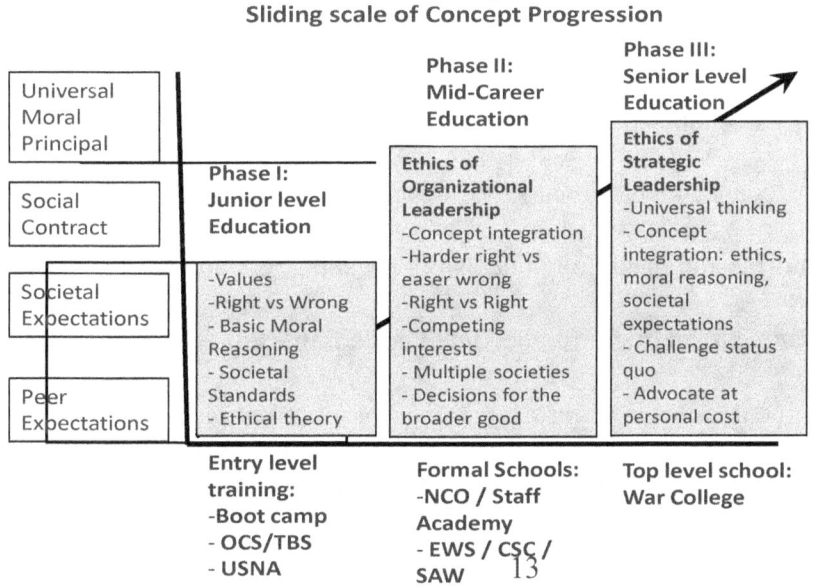

USMC Ethical Development Model :
Sliding scale of Concept Progression

For example, this model would allow EWS to look at its curriculum and formulate the appropriate level of education for its students. This model allows our Marines to develop the ethical foundation through each phase of their careers, building upon the knowledge they will gain at each level and through their military experiences. The model also acknowledges increases in rank and responsibility.

In the first phase, the goal is to ethically ground the new Marine in thinking about the right thing to do. A basic introduction into moral reasoning, virtue ethics and ethical standards educate new members on ethics and how it relates to the Marine Corps. The focus on this period of development forces the junior Marine to think not only in terms of his own peer network, but in terms of his unit and the entire Marine Corps.

In the second phase of this model, mid-career Marines should receive instruction on thinking about moral issues outside the unit's framework and more toward a social contract with larger groups. We are now developing leaders who are developing the organization. For example, the Marine who inflates readiness numbers in order to hide deficiencies in training or preparation is still taking actions for his own self interest, versus the harder, but right, decision of reporting the correct information. Educating officers and SNCOs at this level will help our leaders make better decisions and serve the organization well.

The final level of development would be for senior leaders to handle more complex ethical dilemmas at the strategic or institutional level: forcing these leaders to think outside of acceptable Marine Corps norms and make tough decisions, despite personal costs.[24] The complexities of decisions and ethical dilemmas become very complex at this level, and Marine leaders must understand ethical issues in terms of universal moral principles. A great example is the Chairman of the Joints Chief of Staff briefing Congress on troop levels for Afghanistan. He

14

must make an ethical decision as he explains that the military should increase the number of troops in a certain area because it serves the national interest, regardless of whether the idea has popular support or goes against current media reports. To confront Congress and a politically sensitive issue requires the Chairman to display moral courage and risk career damage and public scrutiny; however, he should put his personal cost to the side and look at the universal moral principles. [25]

The Marine Corps must refocus on what we are teaching and evaluate if we are preparing and educating our Marines for the ethical dilemmas they will face in the future. James Rest conducted a 10-year longitudinal survey on moral judgment and education in 1986. His findings were relevant to the Marine Corps, as he pointed out that education is a far more powerful predictor of moral judgment than age. The general trend his study showed was that when his subjects continued formal education, their moral judgment increased, and when it stopped, their scores plateau.[26] While we know these Marines will face conflict in the future, we are unable to tell them what those conflicts will look like, so they need to have their "moral compass" straight before they go into the next combat evolution. Education is critical to Marines' success, so that when they face a moral or ethical dilemma, they have the knowledge to respond appropriately. Core values and education alone will not suffice unless the training explores the reality of combat and human factors.

Section 4: Training

While an increased focus on ethical education is required in our formal schools, it will not by itself result in the desired end state of a more ethical force. The ethical education has to be reinforced and turned into a habit in the operating forces, particularly in the training environments, so that Marines are prepared to make the right decisions on the battlefield.

Doctors Richardson, Verweij, and Winslow explored the complexity of the military environment and the "moral fitness" that is required to operate in this environment.[27] They equate moral fitness to physical fitness, and their study reveals the requirement to make ethical fitness a habit in order to build a moral force.

The Marine Corps has a formalized pre-deployment training program (PTP) that covers legal and ethical matters. Marine Corps Order 3300.4, published in 2003, establishes the Marine Corps Law of War program.[28] This program requires law of war training (LOW) be provided at four levels, including the pre-deployment training cycle. These levels are the entry level (all new Marines, officer and enlisted), follow-on (formal schools and PTP training), specialized (for personnel responsible for directing or planning combat operations); and detailed (all new judge advocates). Stressed through all of this training are the nine basic LOW principals[29], which include the obligation to collect and care for the wounded, whether friend or foe, and the requirement to treat all civilians humanely.[30] The training emphasizes the four fundamental principles of the LOW: military necessity, prevention of unnecessary suffering, distinction, and proportionality.

In addition to the required USMC LOW training, individuals and units also receive training tailored to specific missions prior to and during their deployments. I Marine Expeditionary Force (MEF) and II MEF administer their own PTP packages for their units during the months leading up to deployment, during deployment, and after returning home. The training is set out in Marine Corps Administrative Message 740/07 (the pre-deployment toolkit) and includes operational and LOW issues.[31] The MARADMIN explains that PTP is a training package that uses a building-block system to ensure all deploying personnel and units receive the full spectrum of training on relevant and timely issues prior to reaching their respective theatre of operations. This order has four training blocks outlined in the PTP, with LOW concentrated in the first block; however, it continues in the remaining three blocks in the form of scenarios and vignettes.

This is required training for all Marines, and all unit commanders are required to have their personnel complete the specific pre-deployment training. This was further outlined in Commandant's white letter 02-07 which was sent to all commanding officers, Generals, and officers in charge, specifically rededicating the Corps to its core values, warrior ethos, and training. While a separate study could be conducted just on what is included in the PTP for all Marines, here we will use a brief example from the I MEF PTP.

I MEF Marines are subject to law of war classes, rules of engagement, escalation of force, and the legality and ethics involved with detainee operations. The Law of Armed Conflict (LOAC), Rules of Engagement, and examples of both would be included in the training. Small unit leaders have a course specifically tailored for their decision making and the law of war. This training is also re-enforced during Spartan Resolve and Mojave Viper, combat training scenarios where Marines are forced to react and make decisions in combat-like scenarios and exercises.[32] Unique to Mojave Viper and Spartan Resolve is a training block called "battlefield ethics." This training reviews the fundamental principles of the LOW, including the assertion that Marines do not harm enemies who surrender, Marines treat all civilians humanely, and Marines do their best to prevent LOW violations and report all violations to their superiors.

There is no doubt that the fundamentals of the law or war are ingrained in every Marine throughout the PTP cycle prior to their deployment. They do go into great detail discussing the ethical challenges in these scenarios, particularly the vignettes. While this PTP framework is

17

excellent, it must be in concert with the ethical educational development in formal schools to ensure the training is re-enforcing or making ethical decisions a habit for Marines.

This "moral fitness" derives from the Aristotelian framework which Doctors Richardson, Verweij, and Winslow explored for the Netherlands Military Academy but can provide the Marine Corps with some utility as well. The analogy of physical fitness and moral fitness is something that Marines can understand easily. As with physical fitness, one's moral fitness needs accountability and standards. One needs to eat well to perform well athletically, just like ethics, where one must be educated well to perform well. Just as one must practice the physical fitness test to be successful, ethics must be demonstrated by action and practice. Finally, Aristotle states that virtue is a state of character and that it can be acquired as a habit. For the Marine Corps, this means a thorough understanding, application, and practice of ethics can build a community of moral fitness among Marines.[33] The values-based training, ethical education, and ethical training can work in concert to develop an ethical culture that will permeate the daily life of every Marine.

Section 5: What Needs to Change

If we truly believe that the most valuable weapon in the Marine Corps today is a Marine and his rifle, we need to ensure that his ability to make the hard but right decisions is sound. Our focus is all too often simply on leadership. The Marine Corps has made excellent advances in its ethics curriculum through the education and training programs; however, it can do more to facilitate an effective ethical force.

Training and Education command, Marine Corps University, and the Lejeune Leadership Institute need to take the lead and incorporate an ethical teaching and moral development vision throughout the Marine Corps — with the structure and formal schools in place.

This can be accomplished in the following ways:

1. **Develop an ethical vision for the Marine Corps**. This is a theme that can flow throughout the formal curriculums and all of our military schools. While all of the formal schools have an ethics education included in the curriculum, they do not seem to be connected or in line with a moral development progression. Using a building-block approach and the model provided will further enhance the strategic ethical vision of the Marine Corps.

2. **Focused ethical education**. Align with Kohlberg's moral developmental model and our leadership continua to create a balanced development, equivalent to the Marine's developmental level at their career-level school. Having an ethical developmental model that serves all Marines and builds throughout their career will create better education environments for Marines in formal schools. If not already established, along with the dedicated technical Marine training areas, ethics must be a core concept all formal schools. This ethical education has to be in concert with the pre-deployment and post-deployment training in the operating forces and these concepts need to re-enforce and support the larger ethical themes.

3. **Skilled educators**. Recruit and create skilled educators to teach these courses at our military professional schools, both uniform and civilian. Some of these educators already exist and are present today at these institutions; however, they are greatly outnumbered, and with added emphasis, the Marine Corps will need to incorporate the increased course load. These educators should be able to grasp the foundational classical ethical concepts as well as modern dilemmas like targeted killings and drone

warfare. They need to be able to teach Marines so they can take these critical lessons back into the operating forces and not only apply them, but use them to educate other Marines.

4. **Shared education opportunities**. Too often, officers and enlisted are separated into different organizations to be educated and trained. We fight together, why not learn together? For example, Lieutenants can learn with SNCOs. Lieutenant Colonels and Colonels can teach company-grade officers. This ethical education opportunity could facilitate the integration and cooperation of the enlisted and officer team relationship that is exercised in the fleet and achieve a common ethical foundation for the Marine Corps.

5. **Moral fitness**. We have physical fitness training almost every day, and we should exercise the mind just as often. We must not lose the gains of our formal schools, training environments, and experience during the daily "garrison" life of the Marine Corps. Ethical habits must be a daily occurrence. Refresher training at the unit level must be a requirement. The Marine Corps must build a culture of high ethical expectations at all times: Whether in Afghanistan or at Camp Lejeune, the expectations are the same.[34] Just as we train to be physically fit, we must train to be ethically fit as well.

Conclusion

" The moral challenges of life come to us every day, in many different forms and in many different circumstances. To meet these challenges successfully, to emerge from them with our integrity intact, we need to prepare ourselves, we need to 'see what it means to be a man who has studied what he ought'." - Admiral James Stockdale[35]

A dedication to ethics training will not only serve the Marine Corps, but also the nation. We will continue to embody what it means to be a Marine, by continuing to earn the trust of our civilian leadership and the American people through our ethical conduct and success on the battlefield. It is not enough to tell Marines to "do the right thing." As leaders, we know we will not be there to manage our forces at all times. That is not how we train or fight. Embracing this dedication to a new moral fitness prepares our Marines for the toughest situations and ethical dilemmas we know they will face in combat. We can do this by dedicating to ethical education in all Marine Corps formal schools, integrating this education with our combat training, re-enforcing these teachings in the fleet, and making ethics a habit in our day-to-day responsibilities. The battlefields of the future are unknown; however, we can better prepare our Marines by training them and educating them in sound decision making. Over the past seven years, the Marine Corps has made great strides to improve ethical training and incorporate ethical education in its formal schools, but it must not stop short of incorporating this fully into a cohesive ethical development plan for Marines.

This refocusing and strategic educational guidance is critical to the future of the Marine Corps. Educating our Marines about ethics and morals will serve the Marine Corps for decades to come. To continue to ignore or reject the importance of training in ethical thinking and moral development is not only irresponsible, it is morally wrong. Providing our Marines with "moral leverage" is the most important weapon we can give them going into combat.[36]

¹ William Stooksbury, LtCol, USMC. *Ethics for the Marine Lieutenant.* Stockdale center for Leadership and Ethics. http://www.usna.edu/ethics/publications/documents/EML.pdf

² Dan Lamothe, *Marine Corps Launches Ethics stand down.* 9 July 2012. Marine Corps times. http://www.marinecorpstimes.com/news/2012/07/marine-ethics-stand-down-commandant-amos-070912/

³ Findings on American institutions. Accessed February 2013. http://www.gallup.com/home.aspx

⁴ Leon Panetta, Memo on ethics to DOD. http://www.dod.mil/dodgc/defense_ethics/resource_library/secdef_ethics_memo_may2012.pdf

⁵ Panetta, 1.

⁶ Office of the Surgeon General, USCENTCOM, USFOR-A, Joint Mental Health Advisory Team 7 (J-MHAT 7), Operation Enduring Freedom 2010, http://www.armymedicine.army.mil/reports/mhat/mhat_vii/J_MHAT_7.pdf

⁷ Robinson, 172.

⁸ Robinson, 173.

⁹ Robinson, 173.

¹⁰ Stephan Coleman. Military Ethics: An introduction with case studies. (Oxford Univ. press. 2012) 2.

¹¹ Coleman, 2.

¹² Editorial, "Ethos and Values", Marine Corps Gazette, 1995. ProQuest

¹³ Marine Corps Core values guide, 2.

¹⁴ Marine Corps Core values guide, 2.

¹⁵ Marine Corps Core values guide, 3.

¹⁶ Marine Corps Core values guide, 3.

¹⁷ Charles Pfaff, *Character, Leadership, and ethical decision making.* (Military Review, Mar/Apr 2003; 83,2 Military Module,) , 66.

¹⁸ U.S. Marine Corps, Training and Education command. EWS Curriculum, 2013. https://www.mcu.usmc.mil/ews/Documents/EWS-StudentHandbookAY13.pdf, accessed February 2013.

¹⁹ Carroll Connelley and PaoloTripodi, *Aspects of Leadership: Ethics, Law and Spirituality.* (Marine Corps University Press, Quantico, VA 2012), 76.

²⁰ Connelly, 61.

²¹ Kenneth R. Williams, "An Assessment of Moral and Character Education in Initial Training (IET)". Journal of Military Ethics 9 (2010).

²² Connely, 79.

²³ Mark Patterson, LTC. Janet Phipps, LTC. "Ethics – Redirecting the Army's moral compass". (US Army War college. Master's Thesis. 2002).p.6

²⁴ Patterson, 10.

²⁵ Patterson, 8.

²⁶ James Rest, "Background: Theory and Research," in James Rest and Darcia Narváez, *Moral Development in the Professions: Psychology and Applied Ethics.* (Hillsdale: Erlbaum Associates, 1994). P. 15

²⁷ Rudy Richardson, Desiree Verweij, and Donna Winslow, "Moral Fitness for Peace Operations," *Journal of Political and Military Sociology*, 32 (1), (Summer 2004), p. 115

²⁸ United States Marine Corps, MCO 3300.4. http://www.marines.mil/News/Publications/ELECTRONICLIBRARY/ElectronicLibraryDisplay/tabid/13082/Article/126203/mco-33004.aspx

²⁹ 9 LOW principals: 1. Fight only enemy combatants. 2. Do not harm enemies who surrender; disarm them and turn them over to your superior. 3. Do not kill or torture prisoners. 4. Collect and care for the wounded, whether friend or foe. 5. Do not attack medical personnel, facilities, or equipment. 6. Destroy no more than the mission requires. 7. Treat all civilians humanely. 8. Do not steal; respect private property and possessions. 9. Do your best to prevent violations of the Law of War; report all violations to your superior, a military

³⁰ United States Marine Corps, MCO 3300.4

³¹ United States Marine Corps, MARADMIN 740/07.www.tecom.usmc.mil

³² Marine Corps Training review,(HQMC unpublished documents).

³³ Richardson, 108

³⁴ Patterson, .p.iii.

³⁵ Jim Stockdale. *Thoughts of a philosophical fighter pilot.* Standford: Hoover Institution Press, 1995.

³⁶ Stockdale, p. 50.

Bibliography:

Counterinsurgency Field Manual. Chicago: University of Chicago, 2007.

Brennan, Joseph Gerard. *Foundations of Moral Obligation: A practical guide to ethics and morality.* Novato: Presido Press, 1992.

Coleman, Stephen. *Military Ethics: An introduction with case studies.* New York: Oxford University Press, 2013.

Connelley, Carroll, and Paolo Tripodi. *Aspects of Leadership: Ethics, Law, and Spirituality.* Quantico: Marine Corps University Press, 2012.

Cook, Martin L. *The Moral Warrior: Ethics and Service in the US Military.* Albany: State University of New York, 2004.

"Ethos and Values." *Marine Corps Gazette*, 1995: (accessed via proquest).

General, Office of the Surgeon. "Army Medicine." November 17, 2006. www.armymedicine.army.mil/reports/mhat/mhat_vii/j MHAT7.pdf (accessed February 2013).

Grossman, LtCol Dave. *On Combat: The Psychology and Physiology of deadly conflict in War and Peace.* USA: PPCT research publications, 2004.

LeJeune, John A. *The reminiscences of a Marine.* Quantico, VA: Marine Corps Association, 1930/1990.

Lindeman, Eric L. COL. *A new technique for teaching military ethics.* Student Essay, Carlisle Barracks: US Army War College, 1986.

Marine Corps University. February 15th, 2010. http://www.mcu.usmc.mil/Pages/CSC.aspx.

Panetta, Leon. "Department of Defense." May 2012. www.dod.mil/dodgc/defense_ethics/resource_library/secdef_ethics_memo_may2012.pdf (accessed February 2013).

Patterson, LTC Mark, and LTC Janet Phipps. *Ethics - Redirecting the Armys moral Compass.* masters thesis, Carlisle Barracks: US Army War College, 2002.

Pfaff, Charles. "Character, Leadership, and ethical decesion making." *Military Review*, Mar/Arp 2003: 66.

Rest, James, and Darcia Narvaez. *Moral Development in the professions: Psychology and Applied Ethics.* Hillsdale: Erlbaum Associates, 1994.

Rhodes, Bill. *An introduction to Military Ethics: A reference handbook.* Sant Barbara: ABC-CLIO, 2009.

Richardson, Rudy, Desiree Verweij, and Donna Winslow. "Moral Fitness for Peace Operations." *Journal of Political and Military Sociology*, Summer 2004: 115.

Robinson, Paul, Nigel De Lee, and Don Carrick. *Ethics education in the military.* Burlington: Ashgate publishing ltd, 2008.

Rost, Joseph C. *Leadership for the Twenty-First Century.* Westport CT: Praeger, 1993.

School, Expeditionary Warfare. "Leadership Curriculum." Quantico, VA, 2009.

Stockdale, James Bond. *Courage under fire.* USA: Standford University, 1993.

Stockdale, Jim. *Thoughts of a philosophical fighter pilot.* Standford: Hoover Institution Press, 1995.

Sucher, Sandra J. *Teaching the Moral leader.* New York: Routledge, 2007.

Thieme, LtCol Donal. "Staff Officer Leadership: Note everyone gets command." *Marine Corps Gazette*, 2009.

Thomas, Joseph. "Leadership for the Long War." *United States Naval Academy*, 2008: 28.
U. S. Marine Corps, TBS Ethics Training. "Training and Education Command." www.tecom.usmc.mil (accessed February 2013).

USMC. "Leading Marines." In *Marine Corps Warfighting Publication 6-11*, by USMC. 27 Nov 2002.

Williams, Kenneth. "An Assessment of Moral and Character Education in Initial Training (IET)." *Journal of Military Ethics*, 2010.